# Hanukkah

### by Lisa M. Herrington

### Content Consultants

Rabbi Alan D. Fuchs, Rabbi Emeritus
Congregation Rodeph Shalom, Philadelphia, Pennsylvania

Carrie A. Bell, MST Visual Arts – All Grades
Julia A. Stark Elementary School, Stamford, Connecticut

### Reading Consultant

Jeanne M. Clidas, Ph.D.
Reading Specialist

**Children's Press®**
An Imprint of Scholastic Inc.
New York Toronto London Auckland Sydney
Mexico City New Delhi Hong Kong
Danbury, Connecticut

Library of Congress Cataloging-in-Publication Data
Herrington, Lisa M.
  Hanukkah / by Lisa M. Herrington.
    pages cm. — (Rookie read-about holidays)
  Includes index.
  ISBN 978-0-531-27201-5 (library binding) — ISBN 978-0-531-27351-7 (pbk.)
  1. Hanukkah—Juvenile literature.  I. Title.

  BM695.H3H48 2013
  296.4'35—dc23                                          2013014853

Produced by Spooky Cheetah Press

All rights reserved. Published in 2014 by Children's Press, an imprint of Scholastic Inc.

Printed in China 62

SCHOLASTIC, CHILDREN'S PRESS, ROOKIE READ-ABOUT®, and associated logos
are trademarks and/or registered trademarks of Scholastic Inc.

1 2 3 4 5 6 7 8 9 10 R 23 22 21 20 19 18 17 16 15 14

Photographs © 2014: Adam Chinitz: 28; AP Images: 19 center left, 19 bottom left
(Kathy Willens), 16, 30 right (Lubavitch Youth Organization/Chabad.org); Corbis
Images/Philippe Lissac/Godong: 15; Louise Gardner: 7; Media Bakery: cover
(Golden Pixels), 27 (Leland Bobbé); Newscom: 19 center right, 19 top, 31 center
bottom (Michael A. Jones/Zumapress), 19 center (Ron Hoskins/KRT), 19 bottom right
(St Petersburg Times/Zumapress); PhotoEdit/Bill Aron: 23; Science Source/Richard
T. Nowitz: 24; Superstock, Inc./Flirt: 20; The Granger Collection: 12, 31 bottom; The
Image Works: 11 (akg images), 4 (akg images/Israelimages); Thinkstock/iStockphoto:
3 top, 3 bottom, 8, 30 left, 31 top, 31 center top.

# Table of Contents

# Happy Hanukkah!

Every year Jewish people around the world celebrate Hanukkah (HAH-nuh-kuh). Special lights, food, gifts, and blessings are all part of this religious holiday.

Hanukkah is a time for family and friends to be together.

5

Hanukkah lasts for eight days and eight nights. Each year, the holiday falls on different days. However, it always begins in late November or in December.

Hanukkah starts at sundown on the first night and goes on for eight days.

# DECEMBER 2014

| SUNDAY | MONDAY | TUESDAY | WEDNESDAY | THURSDAY | FRIDAY | SATURDAY |
|---|---|---|---|---|---|---|
|  | 1 | 2 | 3 | 4 | 5 | 6 |
| 7 | 8 | 9 | 10 | 11 | 12 | 13 |
| 14 | 15 | 16 ✡ | 17 ✡ | 18 ✡ | 19 ✡ | 20 ✡ |
| 21 ✡ | 22 ✡ | 23 ✡ | 24 ✡ | 25 | 26 | 27 |
| 28 | 29 | 30 | 31 |  |  |  |

# DECEMBER 2015

| SUNDAY | MONDAY | TUESDAY | WEDNESDAY | THURSDAY | FRIDAY | SATURDAY |
|---|---|---|---|---|---|---|
|  |  | 1 | 2 | 3 | 4 | 5 |
| 6 ✡ | 7 ✡ | 8 ✡ | 9 ✡ | 10 ✡ | 11 ✡ | 12 ✡ |
| 13 ✡ | 14 ✡ | 15 | 16 | 17 | 18 | 19 |
| 20 | 21 | 22 | 23 | 24 | 25 | 26 |
| 27 | 28 | 29 | 30 | 31 |  |  |

# DECEMBER 2016

| SUNDAY | MONDAY | TUESDAY | WEDNESDAY | THURSDAY | FRIDAY | SATURDAY |
|---|---|---|---|---|---|---|
|  |  |  |  | 1 | 2 | 3 |
| 4 | 5 | 6 | 7 | 8 | 9 | 10 |
| 11 | 12 | 13 | 14 | 15 | 16 | 17 |
| 18 | 19 | 20 | 21 | 22 | 23 | 24 ✡ |
| 25 ✡ | 26 ✡ | 27 ✡ | 28 ✡ | 29 ✡ | 30 ✡ | 31 ✡ |
| 1 January ✡ | 2 | 3 | 4 | 5 | 6 | 7 |

# How It Began

A long time ago the Jewish people lived under the rule of a non-Jewish king. He did not let the Jewish people follow their religion or pray in their **temple**. The king sent his army to take over their temple.

The temple was in a city called Jerusalem. Many ancient buildings still exist in Jerusalem today.

A small group of Jewish people fought back. They became known as the Maccabees (MACK-uh-beez). The Maccabees finally defeated the king's army and took back their temple. They could now practice their religion freely.

The Jewish people fought to get their temple back.

A later story says that the Maccabees cleaned the temple. They lit a special lamp to make it ready for prayer again. They wanted the lamp to burn for a long time. But there was only enough oil to make the lamp burn for one night.

The Jewish people were eager to pray in their temple again.

Then a miracle happened! The little bit of oil they had lasted for eight nights. Hanukkah celebrates the story of the miracle of the oil.

This oil lamp hangs in a temple today.

# The Festival of Lights

Today, Jewish people light candles to remember the story of the miracle. That is why Hanukkah is also known as the Festival of Lights. The candles light up winter's dark nights.

The menorah on Fifth Avenue in New York City is the biggest in the world.

Menorahs come in many designs.

During Hanukkah, candles in a special candleholder are lit each night at sundown. It is called a **menorah** (muh-NOR-uh). Prayers are said when the menorah is lit. Some families sing or share stories.

FAST FACT!

Regular menorahs have seven candles—one for each day of the week. A Hanukkah menorah, called a hanukkiya (ha-NOO-kee-yah), has nine candles.

A Hanukkah menorah holds nine candles. There is one for each night of Hanukkah. The candle in the middle is a helper candle. It is used to light the other candles.

The menorah's helper candle is called the shamash (SHAH-mush).

# Food, Games, and Gifts

During Hanukkah, special foods are cooked with oil. That is another way to celebrate the miracle of the oil. People make potato pancakes called latkes (LAHT-kuhz). They also eat jelly-filled doughnuts called sufganiyot (soof-gahn-YOTE).

This girl is learning how to make latkes.

Kids also play a fun game called **dreidel** (DRAY-del). A dreidel is a spinning top. There is a Hebrew letter on each side. Hebrew is the language of the Jewish people.

FAST FACT!

The Hebrew letters on the four sides of the dreidel stand for "A great miracle happened there."

Some kids get a present on each night of Hanukkah. They may also get real or chocolate money. It is called **gelt**. Some people give to the needy. Many families have parties during this joyful time.

For some families, exchanging gifts is a Hanukkah tradition.

# Make a Handprint Menorah

# What You'll Need

- White and blue construction paper
- Pencil
- Scissors
- Glue
- Washable yellow paint
- Markers or crayons

# Directions

**1.** Ask an adult to use a pencil to trace both of your hands on a piece of blue construction paper. Cut out the handprints.

**2.** To create your menorah, glue the handprints side by side on the white paper. Overlap the thumbs. The thumbs will serve as the helper candle. Your fingers will stand for the eight candles of Hanukkah.

**3.** Dip your pointer finger in the yellow paint and press it onto the paper to make a flame at the top of each candle.

**4.** Decorate the background of your picture with other Hanukkah symbols, like a dreidel, gelt, and a Jewish star. Use your creativity and add whatever you'd like to make your picture complete!

# Show What You Know!

## Symbols of Hanukkah

- Which of these photos shows a menorah?
- What is a menorah?
- Why is Hanukkah also called the Festival of Lights?
- What is the object in the other photo called?
- What is it used for?

## Do You Remember?

Try to recall what you have read. What miracle do Jewish people celebrate during Hanukkah?

30

# Glossary

**dreidel** (DRAY-del): a four-sided spinning top that kids play with on Hanukkah

**gelt** (GELT): a Hanukkah gift of money that can be real or chocolate

**menorah** (muh-NOR-uh): a special candleholder used in the Jewish religion

**temple** (TEM-puhl): a place of worship

# Index

# Facts for Now

Visit this Scholastic Web site for more information on Hanukkah:
**www.factsfornow.scholastic.com**
Enter the keyword **Hanukkah**

# About the Author

Lisa M. Herrington is a freelance writer and editor. She especially loves writing for children. Lisa lives in Trumbull, Connecticut, with her husband, Ryan, and her daughter, Caroline.